NELSON MANDELA

by

Veronica Freeman Ellis

MODERN CURRICULUM PRESS

Pearson Learning Group

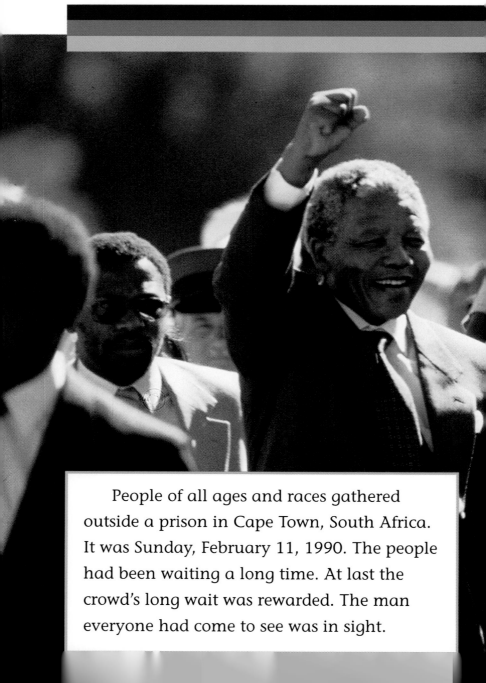

People of all ages and races gathered
outside a prison in Cape Town, South Africa.
It was Sunday, February 11, 1990. The people
had been waiting a long time. At last the
crowd's long wait was rewarded. The man
everyone had come to see was in sight.

With his head held high like a king, he walked with dignity through the prison gates. After twenty-seven years, Nelson Mandela was free.

Mandela raised his right hand. The crowd roared! Liberty for Nelson Mandela! It was a moment South Africa and the world would remember forever.

Nelson Rolihlahla (Roll-ee-LAH-lah) Mandela was born on July 18, 1918. Mandela's father named him Rolihlahla, which means "pulling the branch of a tree" in Xhosa (KOH-sah), a South African language. His teacher named him Nelson when he started school.

Mandela spent his early childhood with his family in Qunu (COO-noo), a small village. In Qunu he was very happy. There he played with other children. He helped with village work. He also learned the history of his people. His father, a Thembu (TEM-boo) chief, and his mother told him many stories about their people.

When Mandela was nine, his father died. His mother took him to live with his cousin, another chief.

The chief sent Mandela to school. Mandela learned a lot from his studies. He also learned how to be a leader. He learned this from watching the chief deal with people.

Mandela learned more about African history. He found out how the African kings had fought to save their land. But the Africans had lost. They became very poor. Mandela made a vow to help his people. He was confident he could do so. He was willing to work hard to make their lives better.

When Mandela was twenty-three years old, the chief arranged for him to marry. But Mandela didn't want to get married yet, so he ran away to Johannesburg, South Africa's largest city. There he came into contact with apartheid (uh-PAR-tate). The word means "separation of the races." Under apartheid, black and white South Africans were not allowed to live together.

The government had made this law. The law said black people had to stay in blacks-only townships. For black people to travel to other areas, they had to get passes.

Mandela found a job as a policeman at a gold mine near Johannesburg. There he saw how unfair life was for black South Africans. They weren't allowed to own land or to vote. Mandela knew he had to do something. He made a vow to end this unfair treatment. His dream was to be a lawyer. He explained this to a cousin, who found him a job in a law firm. Mandela worked there as a clerk.

In 1943, Mandela went to college to study for a law degree. Many students wanted all of South Africa's people to be treated the same. Mandela was happy to find others who shared his ideas. In 1944, he joined the African National Congress, or ANC. The goal of the ANC was to fight for equal rights for every South African. At this time Mandela was twenty-six years old.

Mandela was elected secretary of the ANC Youth League in 1947. Then, in 1951, he became its president. He and others were arrested for speaking out against the unfair laws. When he was set free, Mandela decided he must work to quicken the change in the laws. He was even more determined to keep his vow to help his people.

In August of 1952 he opened his own law office. He asked an old school friend to join him. They were the only black lawyers in South Africa. Together they helped many Africans in the struggle for justice.

In 1956 Mandela was arrested again and tried for working against the government. Other people—155 of them—were tried with him. Mandela and twenty-nine others would be put to death if found guilty. But they were judged innocent. All 156 people were freed.

In 1960 the fight for liberty and justice was still going on. Some people protested peacefully against carrying passes. They were in Sharpeville, a township about thirty-five miles south of Johannesburg. Suddenly a fight with the police broke out. When it was over, sixty-nine people were dead. Many more were injured. They lay bruised and unconscious.

Because of the Sharpeville incident, the ANC was banned. That meant it was against the law to be a member. Mandela and others spent time in prison for helping the protesters.

At this point Mandela was openly opposing the government. So Mandela decided to hide. He used many disguises. His heartbeat quickened each time he came near the police. He was afraid they would see through his disguises.

By now Mandela and his wife had two daughters, Zenani (Zay-NAH-nee) and Zindzi (ZEEN-zee). But because he was hiding from the police, he couldn't stay with them. It was hard to be away from his family. But the struggle had become his life.

In 1962 Mandela was arrested again. This time he was sent to prison for life. But even that harsh sentence didn't kill his hope of ending apartheid.

In prison, Mandela lived in a cell with one small window. It was covered with iron bars. He and other political prisoners had to do hard labor. They crushed huge stones into gravel. They didn't have much to eat. What they did have was often stale.

Mandela visits his former cell in Robben Island Prison.

Mandela was only allowed to have one visitor every six months. Each visit could be only thirty minutes long. There was a glass wall between him and his visitor. They had to use telephones to speak. He could only write and receive one letter every six months.

Mandela overcame these hardships and kept his dignity. He was always polite—even to guards who treated him harshly.

He remained in the same prison for twenty years. Then in 1982 he was taken to another prison. Here, Mandela was able to see his whole family. It was May, 1984. Over twenty years had passed since he had last hugged his wife and children.

Mandela's supporters in South Africa kept protesting against apartheid. They also called for Mandela to be freed. Some supporters weren't allowed to meet in groups. They couldn't talk to reporters either. Some were forced to leave the country. But throughout the world, people kept putting pressure on South Africa to end apartheid and free Mandela.

It was a long struggle. Other governments began to help. In 1986 the U.S. Congress took action against South Africa. Congress stopped South African airlines from landing in America. It also stopped the United States from buying some things made in South Africa.

F. W. de Klerk became South Africa's president in October 1989. He began working to end apartheid. Many people in the government were angry. But Mr. de Klerk didn't let them stop him. He made a worldwide television broadcast. He said Mandela would be freed.

On February 11, 1990, Nelson Mandela walked out of prison. He was seventy-one years old. He had been in prison for twenty-seven years!

In 1991, Mandela was elected president of the ANC. He worked with de Klerk for peace in South Africa. Together, in 1993, they were awarded the Nobel Prize for Peace. They both arranged the 1994 election for a new government. It was the first election in which black South Africans could vote.

Mandela ran for president. Millions stood in long lines. The heat was scorching, but the people waited patiently. Apartheid had taken the right to vote from them. Now they had that right. They were determined to use it.

Mandela won the election. He was sworn in as president on May 10, 1994.

Mandela with the flag of the ANC

Now Nelson Mandela travels all over the world to meet other world leaders. Leaders of many countries have honored him.

Mandela is out of prison, but he knows there is more than that to being free. He says true liberty is living "in a way that respects . . . the freedom of others." He is still working to make sure all people have that respect.

Truly, Nelson Mandela is a man of dignity, hope, and love.

Mandela receives an honorary degree.